Contents

£8-50

NEWCASTLE-UNDER-LYME
COLLEGE LIBRARY

Newcastle Under Lyme College

DC024783

NEWCASTLE-UNDER-LYME
COLLEGE LIBRARY

Introduction

The development of problem-solving skills

Young children's problem-solving skills develop naturally alongside their attempts to make sense of the world around them. When children encounter new situations or experiences, they investigate them using their existing mental, physical or social skills, trying out and refining these skills in the process. First attempts can be seen in young babies learning that if they bang a musical toy it will play a tune. At a later stage of development, they apply their skills to, for example, learning to walk and communicating with others. By the time children reach four years of age, those of average ability and above will be using many problem-solving and questioning skills to make sense of everyday situations.

This book focuses on developing these skills. Individual and whole-group practical activities are used to give children opportunities to carry out tasks that include experimenting and working with materials, learning how to sort and classify information to find answers to simple questions, and finding out how things work.

Early Learning Goals

This book provides a programme that helps children towards achieving the following Early Learning Goals identified by the Qualifications and Curriculum Authority. By the end of the Foundation Stage, children should be able to:
• use developing mathematical ideas and methods to solve practical problems
• investigate objects and materials by using all of their senses as appropriate
• find out about, and identify, some features of living things, objects and events which they observe
• look closely at similarities, differences, patterns and change
• ask questions about why things happen and how things work
• build and construct with a wide range of objects, selecting appropriate resources, and adapting their work where necessary
• find out about and identify the uses of everyday technology and use information and communication technology to support their learning
• use their imagination in art and design.

Baseline Assessment

All the activities in this book aim to enable children to achieve elements of the Early Learning Goals in the six areas of learning by the time they are five years of age. This will offer them confidence in carrying out the Baseline Assessment tasks when they enter reception classes, helping them to achieve results that reflect their real abilities.

How to use this book

The activities in this book are designed to be used flexibly according to the children's level of development. While there is a planned structure to the activities for average four-year-olds, there is also consideration given to younger and older children. There are structured activities that include practical group and individual activities, and photocopiable pages that are designed to

help the children demonstrate and apply their problem-solving skills. If the photocopiable sheet is to be used by individual children, it is referred to as an 'Individual recording', and may be used as a record of achievement or an assessment tool. If it is to be used by a group of children, then it is referred to as an 'Individual task'.

All the activities require the presence and interaction of an adult. It is therefore important that the activities are incorporated in planning procedures and that adult helpers are pre-briefed about the activities and the preparation required.

Progression

The book starts with the children learning how to construct a simple picture jigsaw and looking at seasonal changes in trees. They are then introduced to sorting and classifying information by making simple picture graphs and comparing results. Other activities will teach them skills such as recognizing sequences of events, for example, the journey of a birthday card, and finding out how a torch works. Practical activities include mixing colours, designing a postage stamp, cooking, washing clothes and planting seeds. Finally, the children will investigate the monetary values of different coins and notes.

Finding out what children know beforehand

When planning your work around this book, it would be helpful to find out beforehand whether the children are able to use some or all of the following skills in everyday contexts. Note whether a child can:
• identify familiar objects and colours by name
• sort objects by category and count the objects
• show an interest in observing events and manipulating objects
• describe simple features of objects or events and notice change
• use simple tools such as cutting and pasting equipment
• use available technological equipment such as a tape recorder or computer.

Home links

With each activity, there are suggestions for how parents can help their children at home. If you wish to involve the support of parents, it is important to establish this principle from the outset, perhaps by including information about it in your parents' booklet. Offer appropriate advice through informal daily contact. If you wish carers to help their children with a particular skill, it is important that you share your ideas with them and invite their observations.

Puzzling jigsaw

Learning objective
To build and construct with a wide range of objects, selecting appropriate resources, and adapting their work where necessary.

Group size
Four to six children working with an adult.

What you need
A4 paper; child-safe scissors; crayons or felt-tipped pens; adhesive and spreaders; a simple jigsaw puzzle; a copy of the photocopiable sheet for each child.

What to do
Start by showing the children a simple jigsaw puzzle and demonstrating how the picture is cut up into pieces to make a puzzle. Lay out all the pieces of the jigsaw face up on a table and ask the children in turn to choose a piece and put it in the correct place to rebuild the picture.

Individual recording
Give each child a copy of the photocopiable sheet. Invite them to colour the picture and to cut carefully along the bold lines. Ask them to remake the jigsaw by carefully pasting the pieces in place on a sheet of paper.

Support
Offer guidance where appropriate to help the children fit the pieces of the jigsaw puzzle together, and in cutting and sticking the photocopiable sheet.

Extension
Provide old birthday or Christmas cards so that more able children can select pictures of their choice to cut up into different shapes, and make puzzles by pasting them onto paper.

Assessment
Is the child able to recognize where a piece fits in a jigsaw using clues about the picture or shape of the pieces? Can the child complete a puzzle without help?

Home links
Encourage parents and carers to try a range of different jigsaw puzzles with their children.

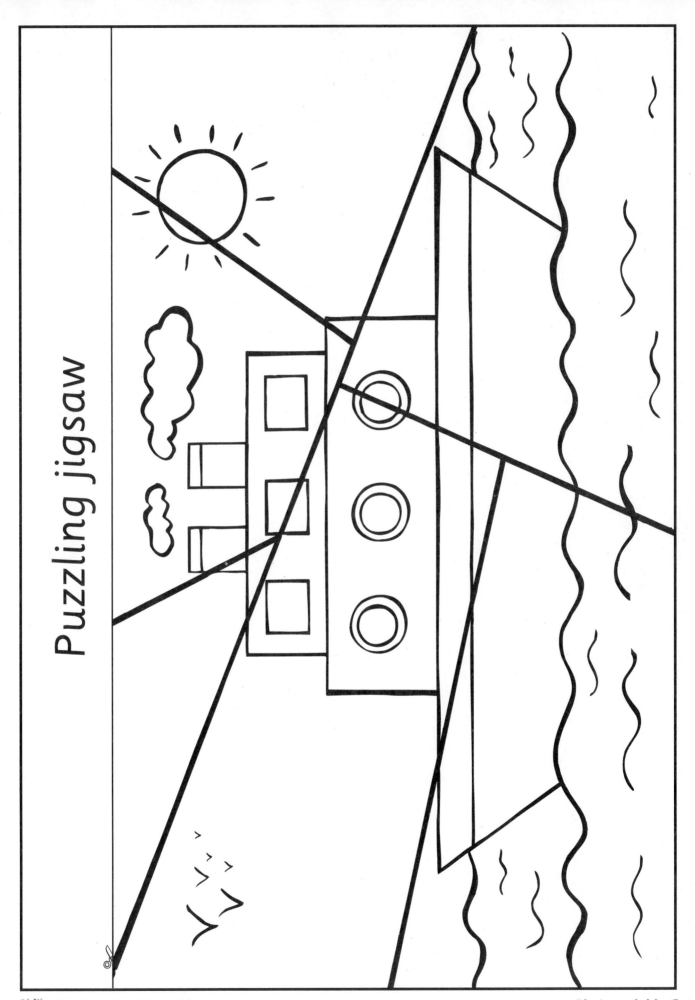

Puzzling jigsaw

Seasonal trees

Learning objectives
To find out about, and identify, some features of living things, objects and events they observe; to look closely at similarities, differences, patterns and change.

Group size
Four to six children working with an adult.

What you need
Pictures of trees in spring, summer, autumn and winter; a collection of small leaves of the same shape; paint; paintbrushes; two paint palettes; small pink tissue-paper discs; adhesive and spreaders; four copies of the photocopiable sheet on A3 paper for each child.

Preparation
Mix different shades of green paint in one paint palette. Use the other palette to mix different shades of orange, red and yellow paint and make up a pot of brown paint. Cover a table with sheets of newspaper and place the materials in the centre.

What to do
Start by showing the children the pictures of trees and talking about the ways that they

change through the seasons. Encourage the children to describe the differences between the seasonal trees.

Individual recording
Give each child an enlarged copy of the photocopiable sheet and ask them to paint the trunk and branches of the tree brown, then to make a 'tree in spring' by scrunching and pasting pink tissue-paper discs on the branches. In following sessions, ask the children to make a 'tree in summer' on a second copy of the sheet by covering one side of a leaf with different shades of green paint and using it to print leaves on the branches. Invite the children to use a third copy of the sheet to make a 'tree in autumn' using the shades of red, orange and yellow paint to print leaves on the branches. Finally, invite the children to make a 'tree in winter' by painting the trunk and branches brown on a fourth copy of the sheet. Mount a selection of completed tree pictures on a wall to make a 'Seasonal trees' display.

Support
Cut out sets of small green and autumn-coloured leaves for younger children to paste to the sheets instead of printing with real leaves.

Extension
Encourage the children to paint pictures of trees through the seasons. Discuss other seasonal transformations, such as changes in weather, animals hibernating, and the different festivals.

Assessment
Check whether the child can identify the seasonal changes in trees and describe the differences.

Home links
Encourage parents and carers to help their child to fold a sheet of paper into four quarters, and to let them draw a picture of a tree in spring, summer, autumn and winter in each quarter.

Seasonal trees

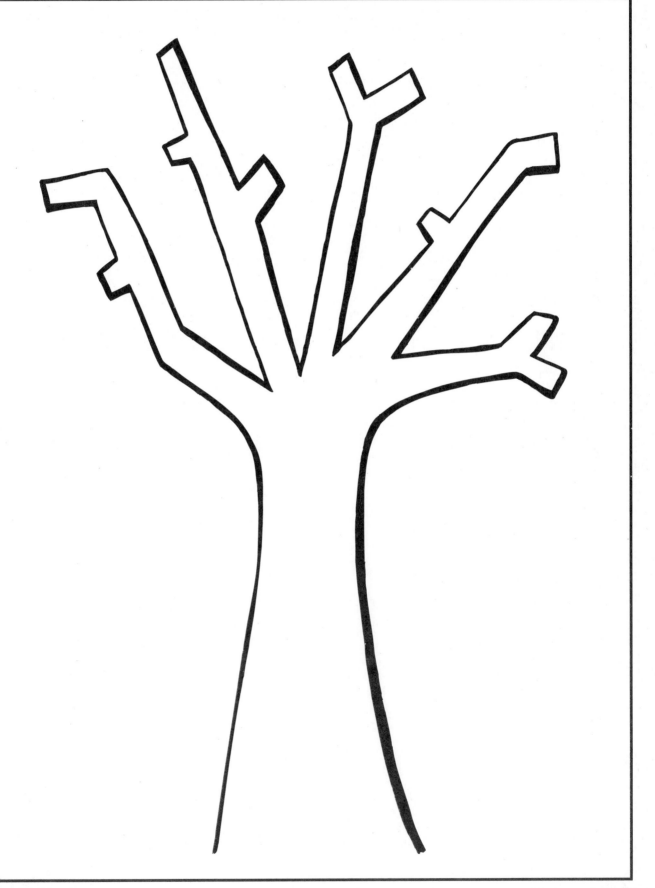

New shoes

Learning objectives
To ask questions about why things happen and how things work; to use developing mathematical ideas and methods to solve practical problems.

Group size
Whole class, working with adults.

What you need
Coloured sheets of A1 paper; scissors; crayons or felt-tipped pens; adhesive and spreaders; lacing equipment; several A3 copies of the photocopiable sheet.

Preparation
Cut the photocopiable sheets into individual shoe drawings and place them in a tray. Write the heading 'How do you fasten your shoes?' on two sheets of A1 coloured paper joined together. Divide the paper into four sections entitled: 'Buckles', 'Velcro', 'Laces' and 'Slip-ons'.

What to do
Sit in a circle with the children. Tell them that you are going to call out different shoe fastenings and ask them to put their hands up when the shoe fastening corresponds to what they are wearing. Choose four children, each with a different type of shoe fastener, to demonstrate and describe to the other children how they put their shoes on.

Individual task
Ask each child to select a shoe picture that matches their type of shoe fastening and to colour it in. Help them to paste the picture onto the correct section of the chart. When the chart is complete, choose different children to count and write the number of shoes in each section of the chart. Ask questions such as, 'Which type of shoe fastener do most children have?', 'Are there more or less Velcro fasteners than slip-on shoes?', and 'If there was one more/less buckled shoe on the chart, how many would there be?'.

Support
Guide the children in selecting the correct shoe picture and help them paste it onto the chart.

Extension
Set up a table with the lacing equipment and a chart labelled 'I can tie laces'. Show the children how to use the lacing equipment and invite them to tie a lace themselves. On the chart, write the names of the children who can tie laces.

Assessment
Note whether the child can name the different types of shoe fasteners, sort shoes into different types, and count and compare the numbers of each sort. Can the child put on and fasten her own shoes? Can the child tie a lace?

Home links
Encourage parents and carers to help their children to practise fastening buckled and lace-up shoes. Suggest that they ask them to sort all the family shoes into types of shoe fasteners and then to count them.

New shoes

The right clothes

Learning objectives
To find out about and identify some features of living things, objects and events they observe; to look closely at similarities, differences, patterns and change.

Group size
Four to six children working with an adult.

What you need
Crayons or felt-tipped pens; child-safe scissors; adhesive and spreaders; copy of the photocopiable sheet on A1 card; large sheet of white paper.

Preparation
Colour and laminate the A1 photocopiable sheet and cut it into 12 cards. Make a teaching chart by dividing a large sheet of white paper in half and labelling one side 'Summer clothes' and the other 'Winter clothes'. Make a copy of the chart for each child on A4 paper.

What to do
Sit the children in a semicircle facing the chart. Talk about why different types of clothing are worn in hot or cold weather, and ask the children to name the items of clothing that they wear in summer, then the ones that they only wear in winter. Hold up each picture card and ask the children to name the garment and say whether it would be more likely to be worn in winter or summer. Choose a child to place the card on the correct side of the chart each time.

Individual recording
Give each child a copy of the photocopiable sheet and a copy of the chart. Invite the children to colour in the pictures, cut them out, and paste them onto the correct sides of the chart.

Support
Cut up the sheets into individual pictures and place each set in a margarine tub for each child. Guide the children with pasting each picture to the correct side of the chart. Ask them to colour the pictures when the chart is completed.

Extension
Encourage the children to draw other items of clothing on the chart, and scribe the names of additional items on the chart for them to copy.

Assessment
Check that the child can identify different types of clothing worn in winter and summer and can place the pictures of the objects in the correct column on the chart.

Home links
Plan a fashion show and invite parents and carers to attend. Ask each child to bring an outfit of winter or summer clothing to wear. Set up a 'catwalk' and provide some background music. Act as a compère, describing each child's outfit as they parade along the catwalk, using as many references to winter and summer as possible.

The right clothes

coat

shorts

gloves

anorak

hat

T-shirt

sandals

bathing suits

wellington boots

sun-hat

sweater

trousers

Laundry time!

Learning objective
To ask questions about why things happen and how things work.

Group size
Four to six children working with an adult.

What you need
Child-safe scissors; adhesive and spreaders; crayons or felt-tipped pens; a child's T-shirt; washing-up bowls; soap liquid/powder; clothes pegs and washing line; ironing board and iron; a copy of the photocopiable sheet for each child.

Preparation
Ask each child to bring a clean T-shirt from home. Prepare tables with the washing resources in an outside space or in a designated wet area.

What to do
Start by discussing with the children what happens when clothes are washed at home. Talk about how some clothes shrink if we wash them in the washing machine. Use the T-shirt to demonstrate how clothes are hand-washed, rinsed, wrung out and pegged on a line to dry. Ask the children to work in pairs to wash their T-shirts and then peg them on the line to dry. In another session, set up an ironing board in a safe area and let the children observe as you

carefully iron a T-shirt. Explain how hot the iron is and tell the children that they must not try to iron clothes themselves.

Individual recording
Give each child a copy of the photocopiable sheet. Tell the children to cut out the pictures and paste them in the correct sequence in the boxes on the 'T-shirt'.

Support
Cut out the pictures and place a set in a margarine tub for each child. Guide the children with pasting them onto the sheet in the correct sequence.

Extension
Set up a 'launderette' in the role-play area for the children to wash dolls' clothes.

Assessment
Note whether the child can name and describe the processes involved in washing clothes, and whether he can order the pictures in the correct sequence on the sheet.

Home links
Parents and carers could help their children to wash a set of dolls' clothes or a pair of socks, and talk to them about the washing and drying process.

Skills for early years Problem solving

Laundry time!

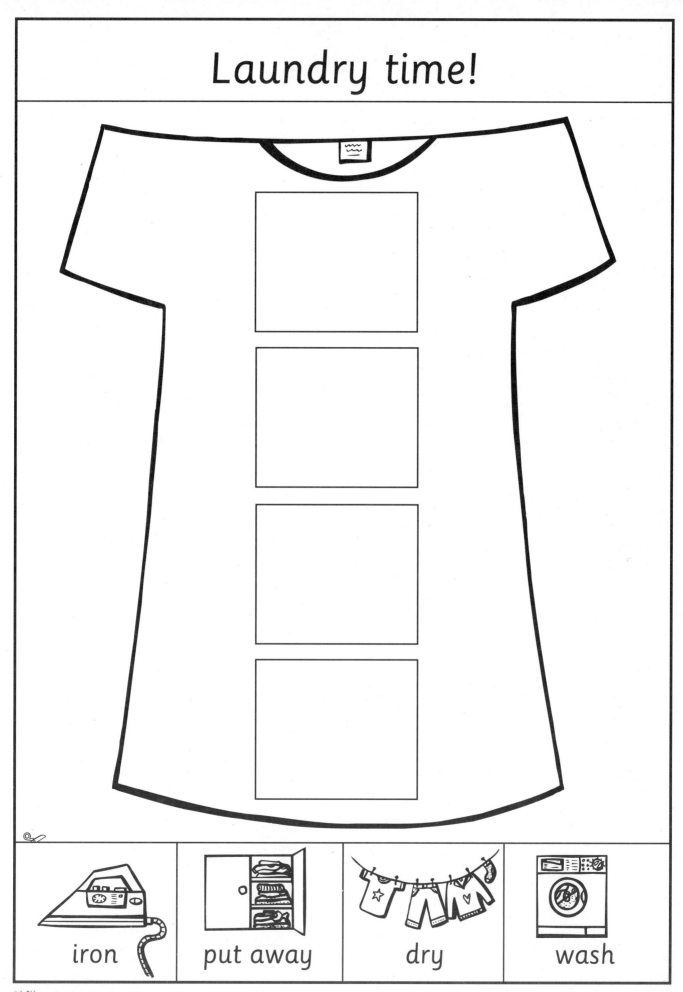

iron | put away | dry | wash

Weather tree

Learning objective
To look closely at similarities, differences, patterns and change.

Group size
Whole group, then groups of four, working with an adult.

What you need
A picture book showing different types of weather such as *Weather* by Sally Hewitt (*It's Science* series, Franklin Watts); six small margarine tubs; crayons or felt-tipped pens; paper paste and spreaders; a large sheet of green sugar paper and mounting paper; ten copies of the photocopiable sheet, four of them on card.

Preparation
For the activity: cut six of the photocopied sheets into individual weather pictures and place each set into a margarine tub: all the 'sun' pictures in one tub, all the 'cloud' pictures in another, and so on. Cut out a simple outline of a tree from a large sheet of green sugar paper and mount it on the wall at an accessible height with the tubs of weather pictures nearby. Label the picture 'Our weather tree'.
For the game: colour and laminate the four photocopied card sheets. Cut them into 24 individual weather cards and secure the set with an elastic band.

What to do
Start by showing the children the book about weather. Encourage them to name different types of weather and to talk about which seasons they are most likely or unlikely to occur in.

Each day, sit the children around the tree picture and ask them to describe the weather. Choose a child to find the correct weather picture and to paste it onto the tree. As more weather pictures are added to the tree, choose children to count how many there are of each type. Ask questions such as, 'How many frosty days have there been so far?', or 'Are there more sunny days than rainy days?'. You could also talk with the children about other types of weather not shown on the pictures, for example, lightning or wind. Continue the activity for four weeks.

Individual task
Play a weather matching game in groups of four. Shuffle the weather cards and spread them face down on the table. Ask the children to take turns to pick up one of the cards and say the name of the type of weather shown on it, then turn another card over. If the card matches, they pick it up and place the matching pair in a pile beside them, before picking up another card. If the card does not match, it is replaced face down and play passes to the next child. Play continues until no cards are left. The player with the most pairs of cards wins.

Support
Play the game with only twelve cards and two players instead of four.

Extension
Make the game more challenging by asking each child to turn over two cards each time. If the cards match, they pick up the pair and take another turn. If the cards do not match, they are replaced face down and play passes to the next child.

Assessment
Note whether the child can identify and name different types of weather correctly. Is she aware of patterns in types of weather – for example, that it is more likely to snow in winter than in summer?

Home links
Parents and carers could watch a weather programme each night with their children and discuss the weather forecast for the following day in their region.

Weather tree

sun

rain

cloud

snow

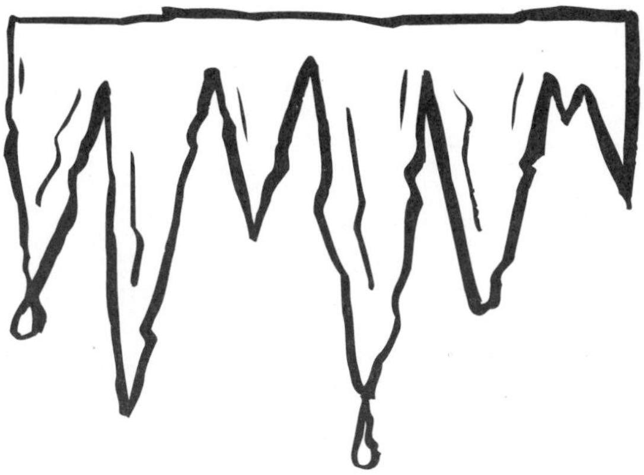

frost

wind

Colour mix

Learning objectives
To look closely at similarities, differences, patterns and change; to ask questions about why things happen and how things work.

Group size
Four to six children working with an adult.

What you need
Palettes of red, yellow, blue and white paint; small brushes; mixing plates or saucers; jars of water; a copy of the photocopiable sheet for each child.

Preparation
Place all the resources on a large covered table.

What to do
Sit the children around the table and give each child a copy of the photocopiable sheet, a brush and a paint-mixing plate. Start by showing the children the palettes of paint and asking them to name the colours. Use a copy of the sheet and a mixing plate to demonstrate each step of the activity. Invite the children to paint the first shape on the sheet in red and to put a small blob of red paint on their mixing plate. Ask

them to rinse their brushes before painting the second shape on the sheet in yellow and putting a small blob of yellow paint next to the red paint on their mixing plate. Invite the children to mix together the red and yellow paint. Can they name the colour they have made? Encourage them to paint the third shape on the sheet in orange. Ask them to rinse their brushes before repeating the activity with red and blue paint, then yellow and blue paint.

Individual recording
Give each child a second copy of the photocopiable sheet. Tell them to repeat the activity choosing one colour at a time to mix with white and look at the result each time. Ask them to describe the colours they have mixed.

Support
Demonstrate each activity step by step so that the children can copy you.

Extension
Provide the children with a plain sheet of paper and ask them to mix two different colours together with white each time. Let them explore what happens when a tiny spot of white paint is added to a colour each time and put on paper, so that they see the shade of colour gradually lightening. Introduce mixing small spots of black paint with a colour or with white. Can children tell you what happens?

Assessment
Note whether a child can name and mix two colours of paint and name the resulting colour.

Home links
Parents and carers can help their children at home by encouraging them to paint using a children's box of watercolour paints and to experiment with mixing colours using the palettes provided in the lid. Children can be encouraged to paint freely on paper or use a simple published painting book.

Colour mix

Birthday train

Learning objective
To use developing mathematical ideas and methods to solve practical problems.

Group size
Whole group, then pairs of children.

What you need
Crayons or felt-tipped pens; adhesive and spreaders; scissors; small pieces of coloured tissue paper; a list of children's names and their birthday months; a flip chart and pen or chalk easel; 12 copies of the photocopiable sheet on A3 paper; sheet of A3 paper.

Preparation
Cut out the train trucks and face pictures from the enlarged photocopiable sheets. Write a month of the year in each of the boxes on the train trucks. Use a sheet of A3 paper to draw and cut out a simple outline of a steam engine. List the months of the year on the flip chart.

What to do
Ensure that all the children can see the flip chart. Let them become familiar with the names of the months by pointing to them as you read them aloud. Encourage the children to join in and recite with you, and to stand up if their birthday is in the month you are reading out (use the register of birthdays to check that the correct children are standing). When you say, for example, 'January', all the children born that month should stand up, and a child of your choice should count those standing and write the number beside 'January' on the chart. Repeat with the other months of the year. Then ask the children to say the name of the month(s) with the biggest/smallest/same number of birthdays.

Individual task
Give the cut-out trucks to pairs of children and ask each pair to scrunch and paste coloured paper around the box on their truck. Ensure that each truck is a different colour. Invite the children to colour the wheels black and to decorate the engine in the same way. Assemble the train, in order of months, on backing paper on the wall.

Let the children have access to the cut-out faces. Allow them to have several attempts at drawing on their own features and to choose their favourite result. Help each child to paste their drawing at the top of the truck displaying their birthday month.

Support
Offer plenty of assistance to the younger children with pasting their cut-out faces on the correct truck of the train.

Extension
Ask questions about the completed train picture, such as, 'If there was one more/less child in the June truck, how many children would there be?' and 'How many children were born in March?'.

Assessment
Note whether the child can say the names of the months of the year and whether he knows the month of his own birthday. Can he name the month which has the largest/smallest number of children's birthdays? Can he identify any months with the same number of birthdays?

Home links
Encourage parents and carers to play a month-naming game with their children. Each time the child catches the ball, she says the name of a month, starting with January. If the child drops the ball, the game has to start again.

Birthday train

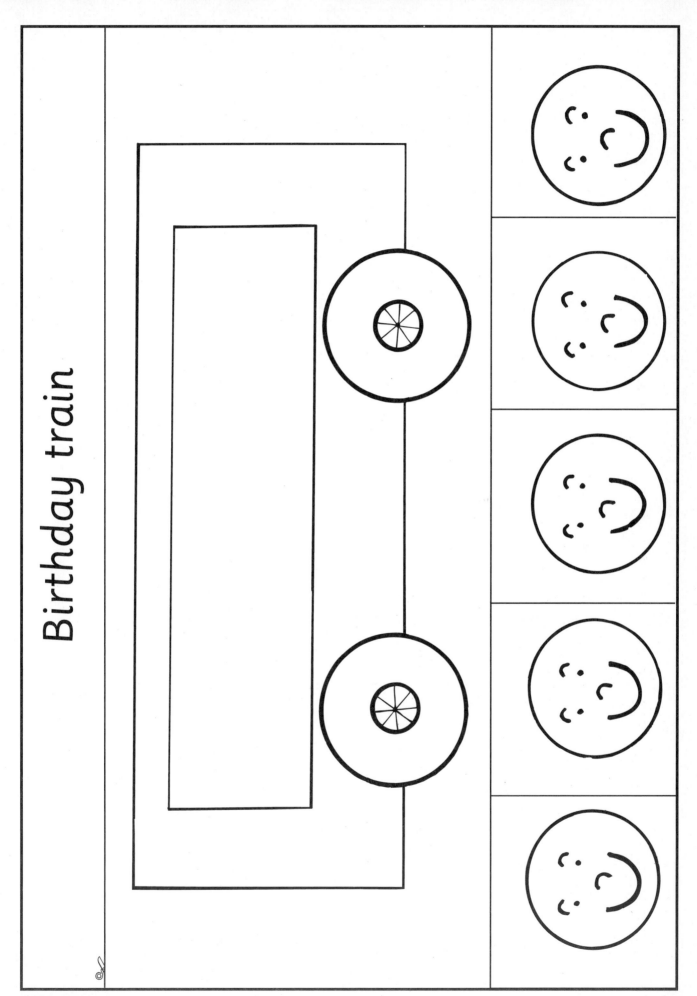

Birthday card journey

Learning objectives
To find out about, and identify, some features of events they observe; to use ICT to support their learning.

Group size
Four to six children working with an adult.

What you need
A4 sheets of coloured sugar paper; A3 sheet of card; sticky tape; child-safe scissors; crayons or felt-tipped pens; adhesive and spreaders; a copy of the photocopiable sheet for each child.

Preparation
Make a copy of the photocopiable sheet on A3 card, and colour and laminate it. Cut the sheet up into individual picture cards and secure them with an elastic band. Cut sheets of sugar paper in half and fold each half in two. Attach four folded sheets together to make a zigzag book for each child (see below).

What to do
Talk about birthday cards and ask the children if they have ever been sent birthday cards by post, and who they were from. Use the pictures in sequence to talk about the journey of a birthday card, from someone choosing and buying a card to someone receiving it. See if the children can recall the sequence of events without the picture cards. Ask what happens first, next and so on, choosing a child each time to hold up the relevant card in a line at the front of the group.

Individual recording
Sit the children at a table and give them a copy of the photocopiable sheet and a pre-prepared

zigzag book. Explain to them that they will be making a book about the journey of a birthday card. Ask them to colour their sheets and to cut out the pictures, before sticking each of them in sequence in the zigzag book.

Support
Set out the laminated pictures in the correct sequence in a line in the centre of the table to help younger children establish the correct order in which to paste their own pictures.

Extension
Encourage the children to look at their completed books and to tell you the story in their own words. Set up greeting card pages on a computer for children to write a message to a friend or a member of their family. Print them out and let the children draw a picture, for example,

Assessment
Note whether the child can identify the different events in the sequence and place the pictures in the correct order.

Home links
Encourage parents and carers to allow their children to stick stamps onto mail to be posted, and to accompany them to put the mail in a post-box.

Birthday card journey

TOWN SORTING OFFICE

Royal Mail Train

LONDON SORTING OFFICE

Picnic party

Learning objectives
To select tools and techniques to shape, assemble and join materials; to handle tools, construction and malleable materials with increasing control.

Group size
Four children working with an adult.

What you need
Paper plate and plastic cup for each child; jug of milk or juice.
Chocolate cookies: microwave oven; plastic plate; kitchen scales; mixing bowls; forks; teaspoons; whisk; wire tray; 225g/8oz butter; 100g/4oz soft brown sugar; 1 teaspoon vanilla essence; 225g/8oz self-raising flour; 50g/2oz drinking chocolate.
Sandwiches: one sliced loaf of bread; margarine; sandwich fillings; Cellophane.
Hats: a copy of the photocopiable sheet for each child; scissors; printing stamps; sponges or stencils; paints and brushes; sticky tape or adhesive; stapler (adult use).

Preparation
Place all the equipment and ingredients to be used on a large, accessible surface. Make a selection of favourite songs and party games ready for the picnic.

What to do
Explain to the children that they will be making cakes, sandwiches and hats for a picnic party. Encourage them to name each item on the table and to talk about what each item will be used for.
Making the chocolate cookies: guide the children with weighing the dry ingredients and with creaming the butter, sugar and vanilla in a bowl until fluffy. Mix the flour with the chocolate and gradually add it to the mixture to make a dough. Invite the children to form teaspoons of the dough into 24 small balls and to flatten each ball with a fork.

Place six balls at a time on a plate and cook them on full power for two minutes. Remove and allow to cool on a wire tray.
Making the sandwiches: guide the children with spreading margarine, choosing and adding a sandwich filling and carefully cutting each round of sandwiches into four. Place the sandwiches on a named paper plate for each child. Cover them with Cellophane and refrigerate until required.

Individual recording
Making the party hats: give each child a copy of the photocopiable sheet and ask them to cut along the zigzag line. Help them to use sticky tape or adhesive to join the two strips together to make one long strip. Encourage the children to decorate their party crowns by printing with stamps and sponges or stencils. When the hats are dry, fit them around each child's head and secure them with a stapler.

Now for the picnic! Choose a good spot, indoors or outdoors, for a picnic party. Sing songs and play games before choosing some children to hand the food round.

Support
Cut out and join the strips of the party hat beforehand.

Extension
Ask the children to tell you in their own words how they made the cakes. Encourage them to decorate their hats using a repeating pattern.

Assessment
Note whether the child is able to name the different types of food. Does she know what different pieces of equipment are used for?

Home links
Encourage parents and carers to help their children to make some chocolate cookies at home. Provide copies of the recipe and a list of the equipment needed.

Picnic party

Christmas stamps

Learning objectives
To find out about, and identify, some features of objects they observe; to use their imagination in art and design.

Group size
Four to six children working with an adult.

What you need
The Jolly Christmas Postman by Janet and Allan Ahlberg (Heinemann); examples of first and second class Christmas postage stamps; real or plastic money; a selection of Christmas cards with simple designs; pencils; crayons or felt-tipped pens; tubes of different-coloured glitter; PVA adhesive and spreaders; flip chart or easel; A3 sheet of paper or card; a copy of the photocopiable sheet for each child.

Preparation
Make a simple display of the Christmas cards on a sheet of paper or card and attach it to a flip chart or easel.

What to do
Begin by reading the story of *The Jolly Christmas Postman*, then choose different children to recall the sequence of events in the story in their own words. Talk about special postage stamps being made by the Post Office at Christmas and show the children examples of first and second class Christmas stamps. Point out the prices on the stamps and ask the children if they can say how much each stamp costs. Explain that we have to buy stamps to pay the Post Office workers for collecting and delivering mail. Show the children the amount that each stamp costs in coins, and explain that when people are sending a lot of Christmas cards by post they often send them second class because it is cheaper.

Individual recording
Show the children a copy of the photocopiable sheet and tell them that they will be creating their own special Christmas postage stamp.

Invite them to think of features of Christmas that could be used in their designs, such as a Christmas tree, a snowman, a star, a candle or Father Christmas. Show the children the display of Christmas cards and discuss the content of the pictures. Give each child a copy of the photocopiable sheet and ask them to choose an idea for their stamp picture. Encourage them to draw the outline in pencil so that it fills the space on the sheet and then to colour the picture in. Mount completed designs as part of a Christmas wall display.

Support
Use a marker pen to draw an outline of the child's chosen item on the sheet for them to colour in.

Extension
Encourage the children to apply some glitter detail to their picture.

Assessment
Note whether the child can name different items associated with Christmas. Can he tell you why we need to buy stamps, where we can buy them and how much it costs to send a Christmas card using a second class stamp?

Home links
Encourage parents and carers to help their children make some Christmas cards to send to their friends.

Christmas stamps

Night sight

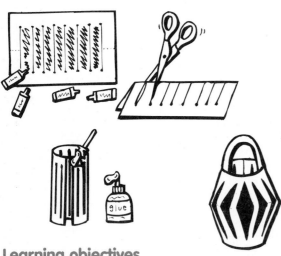

Learning objectives

To find out about past and present events and identify some features of objects they observe; to ask questions about why things happen and how things work.

Group size

Whole class, then four to six children working with an adult.

What you need

A copy of an illustrated information book about light such as *Light* by Brian Knapp (*Science in Our World* series, Atlantic Europe Publishing); collection of lighting artefacts such as a garden flare, oil lamp, candle, lantern and so on; simple battery torches that can be easily dismantled and assembled, with sets of batteries; crayons or felt-tipped pens; child-safe scissors; paper paste and spreaders; 15cm-strips of coloured sugar paper for the lantern handles; a copy of the photocopiable sheet for each child.

Preparation

Place the torches and batteries in a tray.

What to do

Discuss with the children what we use to help us see in the dark and explain that we use electricity to create artificial light. Show the children how batteries must be placed inside a

torch in a certain way to make it work. Set up a table with the box of torches for the children to practise putting in batteries to make them work.

Individual task

Give each child a copy of the photocopiable sheet and tell them that you are going to make paper lanterns. Invite the children to colour the stripes in different colours or patterns. Then ask them to cut out the frame of the lantern from the sheet and fold it in half along the dotted line.

Show the children how to cut along the lines to the big dots then open the lantern out. Help the children to paste the shorter edges together to make a cylinder and to paste or staple a 'handle' to the top of the lantern. Completed lanterns can be displayed by hanging them on a string across the room.

Support

Offer help to any child who has difficulty folding and cutting along the lines on the lantern.

Extension

Teach the children the following rhyme to the tune of 'One, Two, Three, Four, Five':
    This little light of mine
    I'm going to let it shine
    Let it shine tonight so bright
    To bring my friends and family light.
    Encourage the children to replace the words 'friends' and 'family' with two names from the group at a time.

Assessment

Note whether the child can name the different types of lighting equipment. Can she take a torch apart and reassemble it to make it work?

Home links

Ask parents and carers to encourage their children to count the number of lights in each room at home, and to discuss why each light is useful where it is.

Night sight

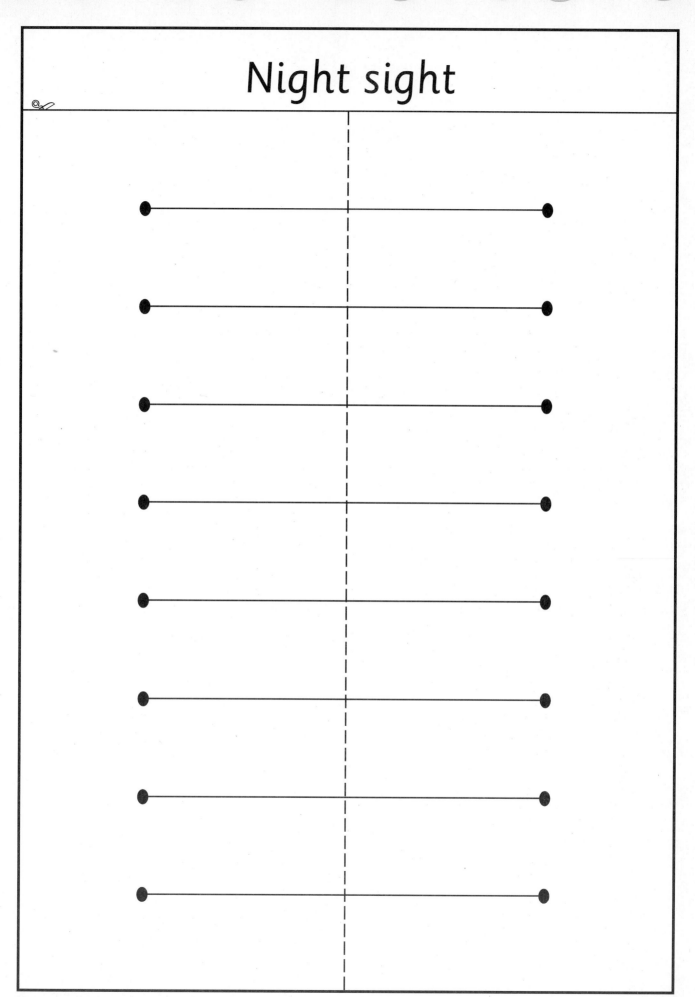

Watch your beans grow

Learning objectives
To find out about and identify some features of living things and events they observe; to look closely at similarities, differences, patterns and change.

Group size
Six children working with an adult.

What you need
The story of 'Jack and the Beanstalk' (Traditional); a packet of planting beans; sheets of blotting paper; clear plastic beakers; self-adhesive address labels; a large planting tub; a trowel; compost; six garden canes; length of string; watering can; child-safe scissors; adhesive and spreaders; crayons or felt-tipped pens; a copy of the photocopiable sheet for each child.

Preparation
Make an enlarged copy of the photocopiable sheet as a teaching chart. Cut off the strip of pictures, colour them and cut them into individual pictures. Place the chart and set of pictures on a table with sticking materials. Cut the blotting paper into sizes that will fit as a cylinder inside a jar.

What to do
Read the story of 'Jack and the Beanstalk'. Explain to the children that they will be planting some beans and watching them grow. Tell them that some of the beans will be planted in beakers to allow them to see what happens when they grow in soil.

   Help the children to fill the tub with compost, push the canes into the compost and tie them together at the top with string. Plant the beans beside the canes and water them in. Next, help the children to roll a piece of blotting paper into a cylinder and place it in a beaker. Place a bean between the blotting paper and the side of each beaker and pour water in to cover the bottom of the beaker. Label each beaker with the child's name. Encourage the children to regularly look at the beakers and the tub, to talk about signs of growth and to check if the beans need watering. Point out features such as roots, shoots and leaves.

Individual recording
Gather the children around the teaching chart and discuss how the beans grow into plants, using the coloured pictures. Ask five children to paste the pictures in order of sequence on the leaves up the beanstalk on the chart.

   Give each child a copy of the photocopiable sheet. Invite them to colour the pictures in, to cut them out and to stick them onto the leaves in the correct order. When they have finished their sticking, encourage them to colour in the leaves. Mount the completed sheets as part of a 'Growing beans' display.

Support
Cut the strip of pictures off the bottom of each child's sheet beforehand. Guide the children with pasting the pictures on the sheet in the correct order.

Extension
Ask the children to prepare four additional beakers with beans. Give two beakers some water, and then place one of each type in a dark cupboard and in a light place. Check these regularly with the children and discuss what happens. Talk about the plants' need for light and water to grow healthily.

Assessment
Note whether the child can place the pictures in the correct order on the sheet and describe what happens to the beans as they grow.

Home links
Prepare a 'Plant some beans' sheet with a list of items needed and simple planting and watering instructions, and encourage parents and carers to help their child grow some beans in a tub or in soil at home.

Skills for early years Problem solving

Watch your beans grow

| leaves | flowers | root | beans | shoot |

Coin matching

Learning objective
To use developing mathematical ideas and methods to solve practical problems.

Group size
Four children working with an adult.

What you need
A collection of all current denominations of coins and notes; a completed cheque for a small amount in a cheque book; an example of a cash card; four copies on card of the photocopiable sheet for each group.

Preparation
Laminate the photocopiable sheets, cut them up into individual coin cards and secure these with an elastic band.

What to do
Sit with the children around a table with the money and cheque book in the middle. Ask them if they have ever watched their parents or carers pay for things in a shop. Can they describe the process? Can anyone identify ways of paying other than with actual money (cash card or cheque)? Draw the children's attention to the items in the centre of the table. Explain to the children that we can only pay by card or a cheque if we have money in the bank. Show the children the completed cheque and then show them the same value in notes and coins.

Individual task
Play a coin-matching game for four players. Begin by holding a card of each denomination and asking the children to name the amount shown. Next, shuffle and spread all the coin cards out face down on the table and explain to the children that the game consists in finding pairs of matching coin cards. Ask a child to pick up a card, name the coin on the card and place it face up on the table. She then has to turn another card. If the amount on this card matches that on the first one, she keeps the pair and turns another card for the next player to try to match. If the coin on the card does not match, the second card must be replaced face down and play moves on to the next child. At the end of the game, ask the children to count the pairs of cards they have. The child with the most pairs wins.

Support
Play the game by spreading the cards out face up on a table. Ask the children to take turns to pick up a matching pair and to say the name of the coin each time.

Extension
Plan a visit to a local bank or invite a bank employee to come to your setting to talk to the children about what they do and the services that they provide.

Assessment
Note whether the child can identify and name all the coins. Can she recognize where monetary amounts are written on a cheque?

Home links
Encourage parents and carers to involve their children in payments for small items in shops, assisting them in counting out amounts, handing money to the cashier and taking and counting change.

Coin matching

Name _____

Skills development chart

I have learned how to wash clothes

I know about different types of clothes we wear in hot, cold and wet weather

I have learned how to make a weather chart

I have learned how to mix paints

I know different ways to fasten shoes

I have learned how trees change with each season

I have helped to make a birthday chart

I have learned how to make a jigsaw puzzle

I have learned about the journey of a birthday card

I have helped to plan a picnic

I have used a computer to write a message

I have designed a Christmas stamp

I have learned about the story of lighting

I can make a torch work

I have learned how beans grow

I can recognize coins and cheques